HireSmart

**Strategies for Developing a Quality
Workforce for the 21st Century**

DISCLAIMER

This book is to provide information about selected aspects of the hiring process and related subjects. It is sold with the understanding that neither the author nor the publisher is rendering legal advice or other professional services. No results with respect to the various hiring tools in part or in whole are implied or warranted, since no control is exercised by the these entities in terms of how the tools are employed or by whom.

This book does not review state or federal laws regarding hiring or firing. The user of this book must be responsible for and familiar with all local, state, and federal laws governing hiring and employment, in general. If a question arises regarding the legality of any hiring or firing practice, an attorney should be consulted prior to the hire or fire.

The purpose of this book is to educate. Although practical advice is occasionally offered, the author assumes no responsibility for the outcome of such advice. Anyone using this advice in any form is assumed to have done so with the understanding that success in hiring is not guaranteed. The author of this book shall have no liability or responsibility to any person or entity with respect to any loss or damage or disappointment alleged to be caused directly or indirectly by the information in the book.

HireSmart

Strategies for developing a quality workforce for the 21st century

How to systematically use cognitive and personality tests in coordination with interviewing and other hiring tools to create a workforce that can compete and win in an increasingly competitive business world

Dr. James E. Gardner

Table of Contents

Introduction

If you are in charge of hiring for your company, and if you have been engaged in this activity for a number of years, it is very likely that you have developed a set way of going about selecting people for your firm. It is my hope that you will be open-minded enough to at least consider the points in this book, some of which may be new to you. For example, we will review the rather weak power of the interview in predicting after-hire job success; by contrast, we will see the surprisingly strong predictive power of intelligence in that regard.

This book is about the four major techniques of pre-employment hiring, with special emphasis on the uses of intelligence and personality tests in the hiring process. It was written with the owner/manager of a small to midsized business in mind. When I first thought about writing the book, I asked myself what a psychologist (now retired) might be able to offer managers/owners who had no Human Resources department and had to do their own hiring. I felt that the answer was a modest "possibly some useful ideas." I did some research, and the result is this little book. It was interesting to write it, and I think it will be of interest and of value to business people who want to improve their workforce through good hiring.

Psychological tools such as interviewing and testing have been found to be valuable in venues as varied as the workplace, schools, and the military. In business, psychologists apply their skills in many different ways. They analyze how systems work, do time and motion studies to measure efficiency, design training programs, and use tests to assess intelligence and personality. Testing has been found to be especially useful in hiring as well as in promoting within an organization.

A principal intent of this book is to bring scientifically validated tests into alignment with empirically derived interviewing and other long-standing hiring techniques. We will argue that the four major tools of employee selection—resume review, background check, interview, and testing—are much more effective when used in combination rather than as stand alone techniques. When properly weighted and considered, the information from these four sources should lead to a "probable best hire."

Why "probable"? Because there is no known method or set of methods that will *always* lead to the best hire. A broad, well-designed pre-employment selection approach increases the probability that a best hire will be made, but it does not guarantee this result. Most employers would agree that raising the chances of making the good hire is a highly desirable goal. If we shift from somewhat hit-and-miss procedures to improved chances of hiring reliable, honest and intelligent individuals, we are on the right track. This is what the hiring procedures described in this book aim for.

What is a good hire? Employers with whom I have talked generally agree that a "good hire" is an individual who is intelligent, honest, reliable, personable, and motivated to learn the requirements of the position and get the job done. The good hire responds to training programs quickly and can generalize from one situation to another. In a workplace, people need to be able to communicate well with one another verbally and sometimes in writing, so the good hire should possess these skills and for some jobs may need keyboarding and word processing skills. Such people make for a quality workforce, one that will be flexible and productive.

The "Big Four" pre-employment tools are as follows:

- Resume reviewing
- Reference checking
- Interviewing
- Testing

The first three tools are almost always used, testing less often, and omitting testing leaves a serious gap in one's knowledge regarding a potential employee.

In addition to the Big Four, three additional concepts can be brought into play in terms of enhancing the harvest of the hiring process:

- Development and use of Hiring Bands
- Linking
- Personality profiling

The four main tools, plus the three concepts just noted, constitute a systematic and sensible hiring approach for most employers. To better understand the concepts of hiring bands, linking, and personality profiles, we will quickly review these pre-employment hiring tools and save testing for a more extended discussion.

The advantages of a high-performance workforce will be touched upon, followed by brief chapters on the relationship between intelligence and job performance, the declining skills of the American workforce, and effective recruitment.

Although many businesses ignore testing as expensive, time consuming, or not worth the effort, we note that testing for intellectual aptitude is and has been a large part of the selection practices of the military as well as major "smart" companies such as British Airways and Southwestern Airlines,[1] Taco Bell,[2] the National Football League,[3] and virtually the entire American university system in which admissions are heavily based on tests such as the SAT and ACT.

You can use the old-fashioned way to hire: put an ad in the paper (or online), interview a few people and select someone for whom you have a good "gut feeling." On the other hand, you can hire in a more intelligent way. When you use the best selection tools, in the most efficient manner, you are likely to make a smart hire. In this book, we are all about smart hiring.

CHAPTER ONE

The High-Performance Workforce

Management consultants, scientists and engineers are quick to point out that today's information technologies are primitive compared to what will be coming on-line in the next two to three decades. Physicist Gordon Moore, the chairman of Intel, points out that raw computing power is now doubling every eighteen months, setting a blistering pace for technological change.[1]

Jeremy Rifkin, Economist

The future is going to belong to people with above-average intelligence. Slow thinkers will be left behind. The landscape of American business has changed at a pace and in ways that few of us could have imagined. With the adoption of computer technology into virtually every facet of home and business, the way organizations must operate to survive and prosper has been forever altered. We are well into the age of information. The advent of the "knowledge worker" is upon us.

Every business must realize that it cannot be competitive without accepting technology at all levels of the organization. From the lowest level to the highest placed worker, an intelligent workforce is critical, yet many companies never seem to consider screening for sheer intelligence as part of the hiring process.

In the age of the knowledge worker, intelligent people are at a premium, and employers must find ways to identify them and to hire them. The old ways of "interview, hire, and pray" are being replaced by the more sophisticated and more reliable hiring tools discussed in this book. The company that has not yet developed new hiring procedures for a strong future workforce is a company that will be left behind.

The term "quality workforce" is often bandied about by human resources managers but is rarely defined. A quality workforce consists of individuals who are bright, flexible, multitalented, creative, who possess good "people skills," and who are amenable to after-hire training. An unrealizable dream? Not at all. When management avails itself of a coherent and consistent pre-employment screening package, the chances of approaching the ideal workforce are greatly increased.

Hiring well sets the stage for your company to do everything well. The cost of good hiring is negligible compared to that of hiring poorly. How much does it cost my company to hire an entry-level employee? A management-level employee? How much does it cost to fire an employee? How much profit do intelligent employees produce for a company? What is the cost for loss of time due to slow learning by an employee of low-average to average intelligence?

Employers need to think about these questions and get the answers. Although I can't tell you exactly how much it costs your company to hire and fire, the answer for all companies is "plenty." The initial cost to the company is the same for a good hire or a bad hire, but the good hire will make money for the company. The bad hire will cost the company money whether the employee is retained or ultimately let go.

For most employers, hiring the best person for the job represents an investment in human capital. How do we determine "the best person"? Let us focus on an aspect of the candidate that is not in full view or on a resume: her intelligence. Your best bet is to hire the smartest person you can find for whatever job you are offering. This is almost always a good idea, though there are some caveats with respect to hiring a person who may be too intelligent for a given job and risk having a bored and unchallenged person doing a lackluster job. Again, screening for intelligence is valuable, and we want the *right level* of intelligence for any given job. Some jobs require at least average intelligence; others need cognitive skills well above average. (That is what hiring bands, discussed in Chapter Nine are all about.) Knowing the approximate level of intelligence required for each job category within the company will indicate the type of training likely to be most effective. For example:

o   Will the individual be able to easily respond to training that emphasizes books, videos, and lectures?
Above-average intelligence usually needed

o   Would the applicant benefit from more "hands-on" training working under direct supervision?
At least average intelligence usually needed

o   How much after-hire supervision is likely to be needed?
A person of low-average to average intelligence is likely to require more supervision for a longer period of time than a person of higher intelligence

o Is the applicant likely to be able to easily generalize from one situation to another?
Above-average intelligence usually needed

o Can the applicant think through situations she may never have had to deal with before?
Above-average intelligence usually needed

o Are the applicant's reading, math, and writing skills adequate for the job?
At least average level intelligence usually needed

Intelligence is like gold: it is hard to find but worth a lot. In every applicant pool there are some nuggets. The trick is to find, hire, and train the best and the brightest. With this said, this is not an argument for simply hiring whoever has the highest score on whatever intelligence test you are using. It is best to hire the brightest workers for any given job category, and use intelligence test results to assess the type and duration of after-hire training likely to be necessary.

Hiring must, of course, start with the pool of available applicants. Businesses are experiencing significant changes in the availability of high-quality applicants, and this problem seems likely to be with us for some time. It will continue to push good recruiting and hiring practices to the forefront. In the next chapter, we explore some of the problems businesses are experiencing because of the declining skills of the American workforce.

Basic Ideas

The landscape of American business has shifted quickly and irrevocably over the past few decades. The age of information processing and the advent of the knowledge worker are at hand. From busboy to delivery driver to CEO, an intelligent workforce is critical for any business if it is to be competitive in the twenty-first century. The term "quality workforce" is often used by companies but rarely defined. For most companies, a quality workforce would consist of workers who are bright, flexible, multitalented, creative, possess good "people skills," and who are amenable to various forms of after-hire training.

The cost of hiring may rise as hiring tools are used more extensively. Even so, the cost of a good hire will always be less than the even-higher cost of a bad hire. The latter results in frustration on all sides, lower productivity, and sometimes firing. The initial cost of a good hire is identical to that of the initial cost of the bad hire; the company spends the same dollars and time on both. The good hire is an asset, and the bad hire is a huge liability.

The brighter worker, other dimensions such as educational background, etc., being equal, will almost invariably be the better hire. An intelligent individual will respond to training faster, learn better on the job, and bring more new ideas to the workplace than the less-intelligent worker. Intelligence is like gold: it may be difficult to find but is worth a great deal. The challenge to a company is to find, hire, and nurture the intelligent workforce.

CHAPTER TWO

Intelligence in the Workforce

A smarter employee is, on the average, a more proficient employee. This holds true within professions: Lawyers with higher IQs are, on the average, more productive than lawyers with lower IQs. It holds true for skilled blue-collar jobs: Carpenters with high IQs are also (on average) more productive than carpenters with lower IQs. The relationships hold… even among people in unskilled manual jobs.

Test scores predict job performance because they measure general intelligence, not because they identify 'aptitude' for a specific job. Any broad test of general intelligence predicts proficiency in most common occupations, and does so more accurately than tests that are narrowly constructed around the job's specific tasks.[1]

Richard Herrnstein and Charles Murray,

The Bell Curve

We intuitively recognize that certain people are smarter than others and that intelligence has value. Most would agree that many top executives are very bright, as are the finest physicians, attorneys, military leaders, and professors. We applaud high school and college scholars who earn good grades and high SAT scores. We often admire people whom we see as "street smart" and who seem to get by on their savvy and smooth social skills. Artists and skilled craftsmen are held in high regard and respected for their different skills or "intelligences."[2]

Given our ability to identify smart people, it seems ironic that many employers ignore the implication drawn from their own observations: intelligent people are highly desirable employees. Myriad studies show that brighter people will generally be the most productive workers in almost any job category. The logical thing for any company to do is to attempt to hire the brightest people it can find, but many companies do not even screen for this asset.

Among psychologists who research and work with the concept of intelligence, there is strong agreement that g or "global aptitude/intelligence" reflects the ability to reason, solve problems, think abstractly, and acquire knowledge.[3] Intelligence is not merely the sheer amount of information a person possesses but also his ability to recognize, acquire, organize, update, select and apply this information effectively.[4] These are the "higher-order" thinking skills.

Because we as a society recognize and respect high intelligence, it seems somewhat odd that all businesses do not follow Microsoft and aggressively search out the more intelligent individuals for their workforce. Even when more mundane or everyday jobs are to be filled, employers often seem unaware of the myriad ways that the intelligent worker, even at a lower-level position, can help their company.

Employers do not ignore a candidate's education, previous training, and prior job experience, and they are aware of strong references and good interview presentation. Perhaps it is going too far to imply that employers are blind to intelligence, because all of these factors involve forms of intelligence. However, many employers seem to simply not value *g* as highly as they might. This attitude is certain to change in the future as employers become more aware of the vast amount of research showing the close relationship between intelligence and job performance.

In *The Bell Curve*, Richard Herrnstein and Charles Murray advance what might be termed the "Parable of the Busboy" to make the point.

> *Being a busboy is a straightforward job. The waiter takes the orders, deals with the kitchen, and serves the food, while the busboy totes the dirty dishes out to the kitchen, keeps the water glasses filled, and helps the waiter serve or clear as required. In such a job, a high IQ is not required...*

> *But complications arise. A busboy usually works with more than one waiter at once. The restaurant gets crowded. A dozen things are happening at once. The busboy is suddenly faced with (setting) priorities. A really good busboy gets the key station cleared in the nick of time, remembering that a table of new orders near that particular station is going to be coming out of the kitchen; when he goes to the kitchen, he gets a fresh water pitcher and a fresh condiment tray to save an extra trip... the really good busboy is engaged in using g (general intelligence) when he is solving the problems of his job, and the more g he has, the more quickly he comes up with solutions and can call on them when appropriate.*

(p. 78)

We may wonder why many corporate executives, human resource managers, and even some psychologists continue to indicate that they feel that high intelligence is "nice" but not all that important for most jobs. Just be "good enough" and you're okay, they seem to be say about their employees. For many companies, it appears that an average person is acceptable. If this is so for your company, you are likely to have an average company.

This casual attitude on the part of some business people about the role of intelligence is often the result of simply being poorly informed about the payoff potential of high intelligence. It may also be, in part, a function of the prevailing attitude in an egalitarian society in which no one is too far above or below anyone else on almost any dimension, including intelligence. It is difficult to face the fact that there are major inequalities among people with respect to IQ, inequalities that can never be rectified. We can say that intelligence does not matter, and we can pass laws against the use of IQ tests for school or job placement, but the fact is that intelligence does matter. Some people are simply smarter than others, and smart people perform at a higher level on the job and in school.

What businesses should do with bright people is clear: hire them. It is less clear, however, how our society should assist individuals of limited intelligence. Low intelligence is going to become an increasing handicap as we progress toward an almost entirely high technology and service society. The service sector can absorb large numbers of people of low-average to average intelligence but only to a point and often at minimum wage. It may be that we will have to drop quota systems and adverse impact notions and work toward agreements that businesses of a certain size will hire and train a certain percentage of low-functioning individuals.[1] The military has been used in the past as a kind of reservoir of last resort for those of few skills and little education, the cutoff point being an IQ of 80, at the bottom of the slow-average range. Today, with the all-volunteer military and better pay and benefits, the services are attracting higher-level, brighter candidates. The minimum IQ has been raised to 90 (in the average range of intelligence).

It has always been difficult to assess brainpower from references and resumes, and the advent of the Internet has made such assessment almost impossible. You don't know who put together the candidate's background material and if it is real or not. Interviews are tricky. We are easily faked out by the glibness of a highly verbal person who "talks a good game." Our problem is that we cannot directly observe intelligence; we can only infer it from the behavior of the person observed. Does the busboy make "smart" decisions? Is he on the ball? Does this executive pick up on new trends and steer his division of the company in a profitable direction? Conversely, does a worker make the same mistakes over and over again? Does this lawyer not perceive the key strategies of a brighter attorney and thereby lose the case? Does this physician miss a diagnosis while a brighter doctor quickly perceives the actions to take and saves a life?

To assess the level of intelligence of any person, we need either observations of a person's behavior over a fairly long time span or a specially constructed, well-normed and vali-

---

[1] In the 1990s, The Marriott Hotel Corporation initiated a program in which individuals on welfare and jobless were trained to work within a hotel framework, the ultimate goal being that they would be able to leave the welfare program. Unfortunately, few of the individuals were readily trainable and the program was eventually abandoned as a failure.

dated instrument (an intelligence test). Because we usually do not know a particular candidate's decisions and actions over time, we need a shortcut. The quickest and most effective way of ascertaining a candidate's intellectual horsepower is a good IQ test. The test score will tell you more about the applicant's potential for helping your company than all the interviewing, reference checking, and resume reading you could possibly do.

Is IQ testing legal? According to the attorneys, for Wonderlic, a company that publishes IQ and other tests for use by business, the answer is yes. Even so, you should always run any assessment of intelligence or personality by your own attorneys to make sure that they comply with federal and state laws. Wonderlic states:

> Two decades of psychometric research and legal development have reconfirmed the importance of testing as part of the selection process. Cognitive ability testing has proven to be valid, fair, and the single most powerful predictor of successful performance both on the job and in the classroom.[5]

Can a brief IQ test predict complex academic and job performance outcomes? How can something like intelligence, now seen to be so important in so many areas, be tested by having a person answer questions, identify the missing element in a picture, define words, make analogies, and so on? Many feel that there must be a long leap between a paper-and-pencil IQ test and the "real world."

As it turns out, the leap is not long at all. The active ingredient in a test of cognitive ability resides in the complexity of the various test items. Any kind of item content—words, numbers, figures, symbols, mazes, etc.—can be used to create a *g*-loaded test. The more complex the job in factors such as information processing, decision-making in ambiguous circumstances, and so on, the more g will be required.[6]

In jobs that require dealing with people, a high level of cognitive skill is needed, because such activities are highly complex and nuanced. In other words, social skills depend on cognitive skills (the relationship does not always hold, of course, because we all have known people who were clearly bright in academics or in business but lacked skills in social situations). A person of limited intellect may be pleasant but perform poorly in a complex job such as customer returns or a position managing other employees.

By intelligently using intelligence tests, you can considerably improve the quality of your workforce as you add new hires. Instead of hiring individuals who are, on average, at about the 50th percentile in terms of intelligence or thinking proficiency, a brief but well-standardized test that estimates a worker's cognitive level can allow you to hire workers at the 60th, 70th, or 80th percentile—a huge advantage in terms of job productivity. Additionally, the more complex the job, the greater the dollar gain in productivity, resulting from selecting top-flight individuals (those at above-average levels), and the greater the dollar loss caused by hiring barely average to average-level workers.

Basic Ideas

Intelligence involves the ability to recognize, acquire, organize, select, and use information effectively. It has to do with reasoning, problem solving, and the ability to generalize from one situation to another. A rough distinction can be made from more abstract intelligence, involving the manipulation of symbols, to more practical forms of intelligence involving the manipulation of tangible things. Both forms of intelligence are extremely valuable to the individual, to the company, and to society.

There is a strong positive relationship between an individual's score on a test of cognitive skills and performance on any kind of task. Test scores predict academic and job performance, because they measure global thinking skills, not because they measure a specific "aptitude" for a given job.

This relationship between IQ and job performance is especially high with respect to more complex occupations, but it holds for virtually all jobs, no matter the degree of complexity. The smarter business person will outperform the less smart, just as the brighter busboy will outperform the less bright and so on across all occupations.

Bill Gates's dictum for Microsoft to hire the smartest people available propelled his company to success. Most companies would do well to refine this notion slightly by creating hiring bands and hiring the brightest people available for the job categories within these bands with respect to their company.

Intelligence is a scarce and valuable resource for any business, thus making testing for it critically important in developing a high-quality workforce

CHAPTER THREE

The Deteriorating Skills
of the American Workforce

*We have students graduating from high school with di-
plomas that they can't even read, who can't write a coherent sentence or do basic math.*[1]

Governor Tommy Thompson of Wisconsin

*… we can teach students how to be marketing people
or how to manage balance sheets. What is killing us is
having to teach them how to read and compute and to
communicate and to think.*[2]

Louis Gerstner, Jr. of IBM

A s we enter the twenty-first century, good workers will
be increasingly hard to find, and a lack of good workers can mean problems in productivity. Companies are
competing for the brightest and most talented workers. Skills
in recruiting and hiring are going to make a significant differ-
ence in terms of which companies win or lose in what will be
a highly competitive century, nationally and internationally.

Workforces are essentially generated by young people entering the job market upon leaving high school or college. In the past, business and industry could be certain that a high school graduate could read, write, do basic math, and accurately follow written or spoken directions. The high school degree for entry-level positions and the college degree for management level positions was the norm. Educational level was assumed to indicate a worker's level of intelligence and capacity for training and advancement.

This assumption is no longer tenable. This is unfortunate both for the young people seeking jobs and for the businesses that rely on a smart and competent workforce for profit and growth. As we enter a time when the need for intelligent workers with good basic skills is increasing, the supply of such workers is decreasing. A few years ago, the Los Angeles Unified School District estimated that 60 percent of new jobs in southern California required "technology literacy" but that only 22 percent of its students possessed these skills.[3]

Almost a decade ago, in an op-ed piece in *The New York Times*, Lou Gerstner, Jr. pointed out that about a third of American businesses indicated that the learning skills of their workers was so low that they were not able to adequately organize the responsibilities of their job. He went on to note that some 25 percent of businesses indicated that the ability to improve their products was undermined and limited because their employees could not learn the basic skills required.[4]

Another author and observer of the business scene, Robert Wendover, states:

> ... *new service industry jobs (which will comprise the majority of positions in the future) will require higher skill*

> *levels than the jobs of today. Few new jobs will be created for those who cannot read, follow directions and use mathematics.*
>
> *Regardless of the size of your organization, these changes (the need for higher skill levels) will have impact on you. In hiring lower skilled workers, for instance, you will discover an increasing need to provide training in basic skills. In higher skilled jobs, the competition will be keener for qualified applicants.*
>
> *… (these factors)… may further your urge to hire any warm body. But with the expense of turnover cutting into profits, staff selection without proper care is not an option.[5]*

An article in *The Los Angeles Times* states:

> *In no other California industry are workers retained, advanced, and rewarded for producing a product that is embarrassingly inadequate, at best. The state's public schools, however, continue to produce widgets (students) that simply do not work.[6]*

The causes of the declining skills in America's workforce are many: the public schools are overwhelmed by waves of immigrants who do not speak English; television has eroded reading and other academic skills; the rise in "time users" such as Facebook and Twitter diverts from the development of basic skills; the large numbers of high school students who use drugs, thus impairing cognitive efficiency; and the societal "drift" that fosters unrealistic attitudes in young people with respect to their own value and their relationship to training and hard work.

The public schools, once the high-quality fuel for business growth and development, are now seen as producing low-grade ore.[7] The situation for college graduates may be almost as grim. The announcement by one large public university in California that 70 percent of its first-year students were unprepared for college English and math is startling and worrisome.[8] Although many jobs may not require college degrees, all jobs are better filled by individuals with good basic cognitive and academic skills. The lack of individuals with such skills poses a serious threat for business and industry.

Until the public schools are upgraded and the talent that they offer to businesses is increased, it may be that companies are going to have to develop their own workforce training programs. If so, prescreening for intelligence and "trainability" will become ever more important. Small to midsized companies that cannot afford a large investment in a Human Resources department can still easily afford the type of quality screening program discussed in this book; one or two persons can easily handle the job. Using good recruitment and screening tools, the small company can sort through the pool and bring in high-quality students upon graduation.

Basic Ideas

Business and industry depend on quality workforces for their success. In the past, the public schools provided a sufficient supply of entry-level workers. The possession of a high school diploma warranted that the individual could read, write, perform basic math, and think reasonably well. An employer could be certain that the high school graduate was "trainable" for most jobs. The same assumptions held for people who had attended two-year or four-year colleges.

These assumptions are no longer tenable. The "product" now produced by the public schools is uncertain. A majority of high school graduates do not possess the basic academic skills necessary to function in the modern workplace.

Competition for better workers will increase as the supply dwindles. Better workers are defined as those who are bright, socially appropriate, possess a work ethic, and have adequate basic reading, writing, and math skills.

Because of the increasing competition for good workers, companies will need to improve pre-employment hiring practices. This means learning to effectively and efficiently use all of the hiring tools available.

CHAPTER FOUR

Recruiting

In the previous chapter, we noted that as late as the middle of the last century, employers could count on a deep pool of high-quality workers. These workers usually had a high school education or better. For the most part, they came with a well-developed work ethic. They were easily trained, knew how to get to work on time every day, and gave "an honest day's work for honest pay." Many expected to work in their jobs for the better part of their lifetime. Unfortunately, individuals with these desirable attributes have become more difficult to find and hire.

Today, an employer can spend a good deal of time sorting through a large number of marginally qualified applicants to fill a relatively small number of positions. Screening using the Internet or by telephone is sometimes used to sort for applicants who have applied for but could not possibly perform in the position. Some companies simply place an ad in the local newspaper.

One difficulty with this kind of broad approach is often caused by the nonspecific nature of the ad. Placing an ad on Craigslist or in the local paper for a position in billing or claims may bring a deluge of applications from individuals who, upon close inspection, are not suited for the job for a variety of reasons.

The first rule of recruitment is to develop a good job description that helps you and the applicant know what the job requires.

Microsoft's director of recruiting, David Pritchard, recommends that, "recruiters attend meetings of units (departments) for which they hire. It helps them keep tabs on hiring needs." Pritchard also suggests that senior executives be involved in hiring because, "If they don't care about recruiting, no one else will either."[1] The executive of the smaller company is likely to be the owner or one of the managers in charge of day-to-day operations and will usually be highly aware of hiring needs.

Wanted: Office Manager for Doctor's Group

A group practice of psychologists had grown and prospered to the point that an office manager was needed. The group placed an ad in the newspaper and also contacted a local employment agency. The group was inundated by calls and applications. The agency also sent a number of candidates for further screening. The psychologists interviewed fifty-four people for one job.

The individual finally hired quit after one week. She stated that she did not like working around "emotionally disturbed" people (it was not clear whether she meant the psychologists, their patients, or both).

Stunned and perplexed, the group called in a psychologist specializing in pre-employment recruitment and screening. The consultant pointed out the following:

a) the type of interviewing one does with a job applicant is different than that done with a patient

b) background and reference checks, though unreliable, are still essential

c) a good job description is critically important

d) the circumstances of the job must be fully explained

e) personality testing would likely have helped determine a candidate's stability and readiness for this particular type position.

This example is not meant to demean psychologists. Far more sophisticated businesses than this group recruit and hire in a haphazard manner. The point is that alternate methods of recruitment might have led toward a greater understanding of the background skills needed for the job and teased out the specific skills the applicant needed to have.

According to Erin Davis in *Fortune*, Microsoft receives some twelve thousand resumes per month.[2] Most companies, of course, do not have the luxury of having so many potential employees seek them out. Even so, potential employees must be contacted in one manner or other so that they are aware of the position to be filled. A "recruiting yield pyramid" may be useful in terms of understanding and using the recruitment process.[3] This program assumes at the start that you will have to sort through the references and resumes of a great many applicants.

How can you find the time to do resume and reference checks, interviews, and tests? Sort through the applications, culling out those who obviously don't fit the job description. Get it down to the final four, invest time for interviewing and testing this group, and finally select the strongest candidate out of this group.

You will find candidates through contact with local high schools, community colleges, vocational schools and colleges. All have job boards and job counselors, and all can do some prescreening for you. You may find candidates by spreading the word about the job opening(s) within your own company. An in-house search may find individuals who have demonstrated reliability, loyalty, and responsiveness to training. Although problems sometimes associated with hiring an "outsider" to manage or supervise current employees may be avoided, problems involved with having those who were once "equals" now being over their peers may arise. Give careful thought to both scenarios.

Candidates may also be found among senior citizens. A study by the Hudson Institute, a think tank focusing on business, indicated that over the next decade, "geezer boomers" will increasingly be heavily recruited.[4] Because some companies have mandatory age retirement rules, experienced older workers may be free to offer their skills to some other company. Research indicates little cognitive decline among the "new old," so it can be assumed that the newly retired generally have retained good thinking skills.[5] The American Association for Retired Persons (AARP) has created a Job Hub as a free service to assist in employer-employee matchups (Google the AARP website).

There are advantages to hiring older workers. They are "work experienced" by definition and are usually loyal and reliable. Older workers are rarely at the entry level, but they nonetheless may need some specific training for a new job. It is always wise to use testing to ascertain level of cognitive skills and, by extension, level of response to training. Given the questionable basic skills of the young American workforce, seniors appear to represent a promising talent pool.

Employment services are another source of employees. If your company has developed a good relationship with a reputable employment service, pre-employment screening can be outsourced to the service. This seems costly, but may save time and money, because the service puts up the ads, does the testing, and so on. However, even when the employment service offers excellent services and delivers good candidates, some further interviewing and possibly testing may still be in order. Employment services are also a source for leased or temporary employees, but know that "temps" do not necessarily develop much long-term loyalty to the company or become particularly emotionally involved in their jobs.

The recruiting process is often seen as a pain in the neck by employers, but it is important and should be approached systematically and carefully. Good recruiting procedures do not necessarily guarantee good results, but haphazard recruiting almost guarantees fewer good candidates.

Once a candidate has arrived in your offices through one of the avenues mentioned, the filtering process moves to the next level. The following chapters deal with pre-employment selection tools.

Basic Ideas

Although high schools, vocational schools, and colleges continue to be sources of talent, there are serious problems in terms of the skill levels of many students. Even so, many capable students can to be found.

Senior citizens are likely to be increasingly used in tomorrow's workforce. Research indicates little decline in the mental capacity of the "new old" or recently retired workers. In addition, the senior group is a rich source of experienced, mature, intelligent individuals who tend to have a good work ethic.

A potential source of viable recruits is the Internet. A Google search for "candidates for entry-level jobs" yielded twenty-three million hits. No one is going to follow up every lead, of course, but the broad categories offered allows for many starting points.

A company's own employees can serve as an excellent resource for new personnel. Because a current employee knows you and the company, he can serve as a valuable filter for people whom he feels would fit in well.

At times, temporary or leased employees may be needed. An advantage to such employees is that they are usually prescreened by an agency; a disadvantage is that it may be very difficult to generate loyalty from employees who do not work directly for the company.

Be prepared to interview four to five times (or more) the number of candidates you need for any given job

CHAPTER FIVE

Pre-employment Selection Methods

*The hiring decisions you make regarding a recent gradu-
ate (from high school or college) is ultimately a judgment
call. You are betting on the future with less than adequate information about the past. As a prudent manager,
with the best interests of your company and career at
heart, you will reduce the long odds by careful evaluation of each candidate's willingness, ability, and potential
manageability.* [1]

A main purpose of this book is to demonstrate the value
to small or mid-size companies of using *all* the hiring
tools, including testing. As an employer, you will almost
always use three standard hiring tools: resume, reference
checks, and interviews. The fourth, testing, is an option for
all businesses but is primarily used by medium to large companies. As we will see, It is not difficult for smaller companies
to perform testing.

Employers who rely principally on the interview in their hiring
decisions may be moving down a tricky path. Some managers
find it difficult to believe that they cannot predict job performance by talking to a candidate for a while, but the interview as

a predictor of after-hire job success is not a particularly strong tool (see Table 1). The effectiveness of this tool is blunted by the fact that many employers (or their designated hiring managers) don't interview well. Employers often overestimate their interviewing skills.

Further, since some people, for whatever reason, tend to be rated as more intelligent than they may actually be, employers are prone to misjudge a potential worker's ability and could end up with an individual who has less intellectual horsepower than had been assumed. If the candidate shows up for the appointment on time, holds a reasonably coherent conversation, and has an adequate resume, a hiring manager may hire a person after one or two interviews, pending reference checks. If testing has been done, there will usually be a delay until the results can be reviewed. This is advantageous in most instances, because it tends to slow things down and gives the employer and her group time to mull things over before making a hire decision.

A hire/no hire decision may be made on valid or invalid grounds. A valid reason for hiring a candidate for, say, a sales position is that all her references have checked out and she is well dressed, intelligent, personable, and at ease interacting with others.

Invalid reasons involve factors that may have little or nothing to do with the applicant's actual job skills. These include being golf buddies, having a social group in common such as a church or temple membership, or the fact that the candidate is a family member (though sometimes a hire in this area is unavoidable simply as a means of keeping peace in the family).

These reasons may blind when making an important hiring decision.

Interview, resumes, and reference checks are not particularly strong predictors of after-hire job performance. When testing is added, however, the predictive power of the combination goes up, especially because the best predictor of after-hire job performance is the candidate's score on an intelligence test (see Table 1). This statement is somewhat counterintuitive and seems so amazing to some managers that they have difficulty accepting it. Employers tend to assume that if they interview well and the resumes look okay, they are making good hires, and they might be. However, they could raise their chances by adding testing for intelligence.

The concept of intelligence or IQ has not been in favor in this country for years, this partially having to do with the fact that we, as a people, have some difficulty with the notion of a "meritocracy" based on intelligence. The whole story, though fascinating, is well beyond the purview of this book. Suffice it to say that an intelligent workforce is like money in the bank. Poets tell us that a rose is a rose by whatever name, coaches say that sheer speed in most sports is desirable, and common sense tells us that smart employees can help our business. Intelligence is a "value-added" dimension.

The common-sense assumption of many employers ("An interview is the best predictor of job performance") is contradicted by research findings. Table 1 compares the most frequently used predictors of after-hire job success.

Table 1

The Validity of Different Predictors of Job Performance [2]

Predictor of job performance	Validity score*
Intelligence test score	.53
Resume	.37
Reference checks	.26
Education	.22
Interview	.14
College grades	.11
Expressed interest in the job	.10

* The higher the number, the better the prediction of job performance.

A validity score of .53 for an intelligence test means that intelligence or "cognitive skills" is at the top of the list of pr-employment tools in terms of being able to predict after-hire success on the job. Intelligence is a good predictor, though far from perfect. The .53 validity coefficient means that intelligence is accounting for about 28 percent of the variance involved in predicting job performance (the validity coefficient squared provides the amount of variation accounted for on that particular dimension). Thus, the IQ score will provide between one-quarter and one-third of the predictive power on a job hire. The other 72 percent or so derives from other factors such as drive, interpersonal skills, background experience, education, and so on.

As can be seen, the interview comes in fifth among the tools of selection in terms of ability to predict after-hire job performance. This finding is surprising to some. However, with a little training, any of us can sharpen our interviewing techniques. Our skills might even move to the top of the list under certain circumstances.

The best predictor of future job behavior is probably past job behavior, if the new job is similar to the old one. Thus, the resume must be given considerable weight. On the other hand, if the candidate will be asked to enter a training program on the new job and learn new skills, we come back to a strong reliance on intelligence.

Intelligence involves not only "book smarts" but also the ability to adapt creatively and effectively to new problems. New jobs create new problems that require developing new sets of behaviors and new thinking patterns. Intelligent people generally respond well to the pressures and demands of new problems, and they respond well to training procedures. Intelligent people learn quickly, deal with complexity well, and often add new tactics to old procedures. [3]

Let us be clear about intelligence. We like the brilliant "nerds" from Cal Tech and MIT, but we are not talking about this group. We are underlining the value of the "regular" worker who is of above-average general intelligence (that ubiquitous g factor). The candidate still has to interview well, possess a good resume, pass reference checks, be honest and reliable, and have the requisite personality for the job.

As every business owner or manager knows, you can still go wrong even if you do everything right. The small company winners in the twenty-first century will be those smart enough to recognize the value of bringing into focus all four hiring tools. A quality workforce is the product of management's intelligent use of the available hiring strategies.

Basic Ideas

The four pre-employment selection methods, in order of their usual use, are resume or application review, reference checks, interviews, and testing. The first three are used by almost all companies; the fourth, testing, is underused.

To get the best hires for your company, these selection tools need to be used in a systematic and coordinated way. They will generate considerable data that will need to be linked and focused.

Laws restrict many aspects of pre-employment screening. It is important that the employer be aware of every aspect of these laws. This is a "how to hire" book and does not purport to cover the laws regulating hiring (or firing). Employers should approach each hiring situation carefully, assuming that all who apply for the job are eligible regardless of age, sex, religion, national origin, disability, physical appearance or marital status. Even with the existence of possible restrictions, a company should be very proactive in hiring and attempt to acquire the best worker from the talent pool while exercising due diligence with respect to relevant laws. This book does not offer legal advice and an attorney should be consulted with respect to your company's hiring procedures.

There are valid and invalid reasons for making a hire. Invalid reasons involve emotional ties such as those found in "the old boy's network" and those involving family. These are the ties that blind and they reduce objectivity. Valid reasons for hiring will always involve getting the individual whose intelligence, personal skills, and experience make that individual the best person for the job.

CHAPTER SIX

The Resume

The resume ranks second as the most effective predictor of after-hire job performance [1], but is the information accurate?

The resume provides an overview of a candidate's background. It is usually required for middle and upper-level management positions (background material on the job application generally suffices for entry-level positions). The resume relates what the candidate *wants* to tell about what he has done and where he has been. When truthful, they are invaluable, but in the hands of a good liar, they are a huge problem for business. Websites exist that will help a candidate falsify some or all of his background. They can put a good spin on some aspects of the person's background and delete other aspects altogether.

You, or your background fact checker, can sometimes get around these bogus services. If you personally know someone in a company referenced on a resume, you make a direct contact with that individual and validate the information.

Business people with considerable hiring experience say that they know what to look for on an application or in a resume.

They look at the appearance of the envelope or the email, then the cover letter, if there is one, and then the resume itself. These are, after all, important samples of the candidate's work product. It shows the standards to which he holds himself and is willing to present to others. It follows adage of "first impressions are lasting impressions," and we all know that you only get one chance to make a good first impression. If the cover letter is not brief and to the point or contains misspelling and errors in grammar, these indicate limited writing skills or possibly a careless applicant.

Even employers experienced in hiring will sometimes review resumes that have clearly been professionally produced by a resume writing service. The resume may be over-expanded, verging on being a tall tale. The candidate might still be worth interviewing, however. The professionally produced resume, at a minimum, indicates that the applicant cared enough and was smart enough to hire someone to help make his background more presentable and professional.

A candidate with a poor resume is probably not the person to hire, since what you see is probably what you will get when he is on the job. If the candidate has not grasped the importance of a crisp, clean resume, he is not likely to "get it" in other areas of his work.

I recently served as an examiner for a psychologist seeking Diplomate status. The Diplomate is the highest professional degree that can be accorded, and one must have earned a PhD from an accredited university for at least five years prior to sitting for this exam. As part of the evaluation, the doctor must present a work sample. As I reviewed this person's work sample, I was amazed to see that it was presented in a loose-leaf binder, typed instead of word processed, and erroneous or misspelled words were marked out instead of replaced. It was a shoddy, careless piece of work. The rest of the doctor's clinical work in the exam was equally haphazard. He did not pass the exam.

The following letter appeared in the "Ask Amy" column of the March 1, 2011 edition of *The Los Angeles Times*:

New Resumes Are Sloppy

Dear Amy, My partner and I run a small business and are currently in the process of hiring employees.

We have asked candidates to fill out an application and to send us their resumes via e-mail. Although we do not expect perfection, the errors on the applications we have received are astonishing: incomplete sentences, numerous spelling errors, format inconsistencies, and an absence of periods and capitalization.

Most of our applicants are recent college graduates. Although perfect grammar is not a requirement of this position, attention to detail is important. We want to say something to our applicants to encourage them to take more time on future job applications. Making a good first impression is important. However, we aren't sure that this is our place. If we speak up, how should we approach the topic in a professional, nonthreatening way.

Conflicted

Dear Conflicted: It is not your duty to educate these rookie applicants, but you would be doing them a favor—as well as conveying your company's expectations and image—by attaching very simple instructions before you invite them to apply.

> *Your letter should say something like, "We look forward to learning more about you. Keep in mind, however, that the application is your first opportunity to impress us. Please use special care with your writing, spelling, grammar and format. Those applications that don't conform to a basic standard will not make it past the first cut."*

When looking over a candidate's resume or application, consider the timeline. Has the candidate remained at one company for a long time, or has he jumped from job to job? If the latter, why? If the former, why is he choosing to leave now?

In the process of reviewing the candidate's background, you will see what information he provided regarding his education. Education is the fourth-best predictor of job performance. However, like reference checks and resumes, this data can be falsified, sometimes blatantly. You may find outright lies about graduating from a particular college or some "spin" about grades, honors, or awards. (In the movie *Catch Me If You Can*, Leonardo de Caprio entertained viewers with his chameleon-like facile changes of phony occupations and backgrounds.) This kind of person can apply to any business.

Reviewing numerous resumes can be a boring task, but the information gleaned is valuable. One manager stated:

> *It (reviewing resumes or applications) can be tedious and time consuming. But, the information in them is obviously useful to us if for nothing else than obtaining the applicant's phone number, address and social security number. We use an application form here but people send in resumes, too. I'm the one who reads them all initially. Our standard form application is usually sufficient for our needs.*

My plant manager, my bookkeeper and my wife also read applications that I have given an initial "possibly okay" to. One or two of us will then do a quick interview with the applicant. I've read about more extensive interviewing techniques but we usually don't have time. I'd love to do some testing but, again, we don't have time and don't really know how to go about it.

We used to do pretty careful reference checks but not so much now. You end up playing a lot of telephone tag, though e-mails can help. Also, no one will talk too openly with you about a former employee because of fear of litigation. And we are no better. We don't usually tell all about someone who has left us or we have let go, regardless of the reason. We've all become timid about the use of negative information.

An experienced employer can, in theory, use the resume to construct a picture of who the applicant is. The resume/application tells a story, and it is worth taking time to "read" the story by studying the information carefully. You might see a work history with gaps, which may mean something has been left out, or with leaps, which may indicate promotions. Time spent reviewing the information the candidate has provided is worth your while. The resume is a valuable tool, because it will be one of the better predictors of job performance.

Basic Ideas

The resume and the reference check rank high on the list of predictors for after-hire job success when they are truthful. These are both essentially work histories. Resumes are usually required of management-level applicants; the application form is standard for lower entry-level positions.

A work history is a good bet as a predictor for future job success if the person's previous job is similar to the job for which he is applying. If the jobs are not similar, the predictive power of the work history declines. The candidate's educational level is the fourth-best predictor of after-hire job success as it is highly correlated with intelligence.

A major problem with all background material is the ease of falsification. There are now companies that specialize in such falsification, even to the extent of replying to a prospective employer's phone calls and "verifying" fictitious information. Even so, the resume/application will continue to be used.

In any case, the employer should be alert to the aspects that indicate important characteristics of the candidate: presentation, neatness, writing ability, and spelling.

CHAPTER SEVEN

Checking References

How much information can you get from contacting the applicant's previous employer? Sometimes a lot, and sometimes almost none. Because of the often-haphazard procedures used by many businesses in checking references, key information may be missing, information that you could have obtained by asking a few more questions. Unfortunately, in a litigious climate, employers are sometimes reluctant to be frank about former employees. Even so, you should carefully check references, because this represents due diligence on your part and can help to mitigate difficulties with a worker who later proves to be a problem. With the candidate's permission, check the references provided. [1]

A perfect predictor would indicate exactly whether or not a given individual was going to work out well on the job. What a tool *that* would be! Unfortunately, no such tool exists. Reference checks predict at about a 7 percent level (resumes at about a 14 percent level, intelligence tests at about a 28 percent level). Even though the performance prediction provided by a reference check is low, it is still a valuable tool when used with the other predictors and should be performed as part of due diligence. Set aside time specifically for checking references with care.

Check references as soon as possible. If you get negative feedback right away, you can stop the screening process at that point and save yourself time and money. As indicated, some employers fear legal consequences if they speak negatively about a former employee. A clever applicant might contact a past employer and attempt to ascertain what kind of reference will be given. If it is negative, she might leave that employer off her list of references. This is why it is important to look for gaps in the employment history. While some companies only verify dates of employment without further comment, fitting dates of employment into the applicant's work history timeline is useful in itself.

Susan Dearmin of Accountemps in Woodland Hills, California, offers some excellent suggestions that help to maximize the value of reference checks. [2] She advises the following:

> Don't delegate the process. With the exception of complicated background checks, the person making the hiring decision is the one who should check the references.

> Before you make the first call, have a clear idea of the question you intend to ask. Try to strike a balance between specific information questions (How long did Sam Jones work for you?) and inquiries designed to verify or challenge whatever general impressions you may have (already formed) about the candidate.

> The list of references provided by job applicants often consists of people who have been "briefed" by the candidate, so they may not be completely objective. To reach a broader range of individuals, ask the candidate during

*the interview for additional names. Then 'network' your
way to other people who know the applicant.*

*Don't forget to use other sources of information such as
people who may belong to the same professional association as the candidate, and search among your industry
contacts for people who may know the individual. Keep
in mind that you are not necessarily looking for detailed
information. You're listening for clues that could shed
light on what you learned during the interview process.*

*Finally, include a question (or two) to determine the can-
dor and validity of the person giving the reference. A
good way to do this is to ask a question to which you
already know the answer.*

You should use a set of standardized questions as a basic
framework, but you can and should follow up on any lead and
go where the conversation takes you. Remember, you can *ask*
only job-related questions, but you can *listen* to whatever the
candidate might want to say about anything in her life: previous employment, marriage, children, leisure, and so on.

When speaking with a former employer, use open-ended
questions to ascertain if the employer provides the same
information the candidate has given. For example, you might
ask, "What period of time did Mr. Doe work for you?" instead
of, "Did Mr. Doe work for you from September 2005 to June
2007?"

Other questions might involve the candidate's attitude toward
her work and whether she was reliable. Always ask a previous
employer if she would hire this applicant again. If the candidate has told you her reason for leaving the previous company, you can ascertain whether the company sees things the
same way. Ask about duties and responsibilities. Leave your

questions open-ended when you can. (If you are not used to asking these kinds of questions, rehearse them on your own or with a colleague.) A simple list of standardized questions might involve four or five "when, what, and where" questions. Crosscheck the answers against information the applicant has provided in her resume and interview.

A key question is, "Would you hire this person for that position again?" An unqualified "yes" tells you a lot, and a qualified "perhaps" provides much information if you read between the lines of the response. Although a "no" response would seem to close the book on the candidate, this may not be quite the case. If the previous employer would not hire the person again under any circumstances, you might find out what happened. There may be some mitigating factors. The previous employer may be indicating that the applicant was a good employee in many ways but did not work out well in that particular position and that she might be considered for some other position. You don't want to give up too easily on a potentially good worker. Good people are too hard to find.

Listen carefully to what previous employers say about the candidate. Tone of voice is important. A sarcastic, "What a worker," from a previous employer tells you a lot about the candidate. Set aside time to make these calls and thinks about what you have (or have not) been told about the candidate. It is a boring thing to do and most of tend to rush through these calls. When we do this, we are just wasting our time and the time of whomever we are calling.

A friend of mine who owns a business with fifty or so employees allowed me to listen in on one of his reference check calls. My notes are as follows:

Hello. My name is _____. I'm the owner of Widget Company, and I'm calling about a former employee of yours, Ms._____. Could you tell me a bit about her? (Listens for a few minutes.) It sounds like she was okay for you. You liked her work okay. She was on time and at work most of the time. And her job for you was inventory control? Not exactly the manager? But she worked in that department for almost a year. Was her work okay? Okay and thanks. Lunch on me soon, okay?"

My friend got some facts about the applicant, but he did not get a complete picture. After we discussed his somewhat haphazard approach, my friend decided that he would tighten up his approach to reference checks. I referred him to Susan Dearmin's excellent article noted above.

If employers were to conduct more focused reference checks, it is likely that the 7 percent success rate for job prediction would rise considerably. The reference check as a predictor seems to be poor primarily because the reference check, itself, is often poorly done and, of course, because previous employers are guarded in what they feel they can tell you.

While accurate information about the applicant is critical to an employer making a hiring decision, many job seekers count on the fact that few references at any level are ever checked. As a result, we have doctors who are not doctors, managers who have never managed, marriage counselors who have never passed the relevant exams, and so on.

As troublesome as it can sometimes be, the reference check can provide important pieces of information for the employer to integrate with interview material, the resume, and the test results as he moves toward selecting a well-qualified worker.

Basic Ideas

References are the third-best indicators of after-hire job performance. Checking references is an exercise in due diligence, especially with regard to any problem behavior in the workplace.

Even though many former employers are reluctant to be frank because of the current climate of litigation, you can at least show that you made an honest effort to evaluate the candidate's past.

Anything less than a "yes" answer to the question, "Would you hire this person for the same position again?" should cause you to explore the reason for the response.

A good approach is to develop a set of standardized questions to ask about each candidate. Don't delegate the process of reference checking. In most cases, the person doing the hiring should be doing the reference checking.

CHAPTER EIGHT

The Interview

"Listen, think, respond. It is the hardest kind of work, but worth the effort."[1]

Dr. L. E. Tyler

Psychologist and interviewing specialist

The interview is an attempt to predict job performance by talking with the candidate. Although the interview is not highly ranked as a predictor of job performance, it is still important, and no employer is likely to stop interviewing applicants. Employers and managers understandably want to talk with the applicant before offering him a job. From this contact, the employer attempts to ascertain whether or not he and the applicant can get along with one another and with other employees.

The more similar the candidate's previous job to the position for which he is applying, the better his fit will be in the new job. The interviewer has to understand the demands of the job and carefully evaluate the fit between the old one and the new one. Cold-call selling, for example, is different from selling to walk-in customers, though both come under the category of sales.

The interviewer may find that there is little similarity between the applicant's job experience and the position for which he is applying, even though his resume indicated otherwise. However, if the applicant impressively demonstrates desirable qualities such as a pleasing personality and good verbal skills, the employer might consider making a probational hire.

Every interview is an interaction between the employer and the applicant. The psychologist, Arthur Wiens, notes, "Both participants share actively in the process of interviewing, and both participants are influenced by each other; the end product of the interview is a result of this interaction."[2] Choosing the appropriate person within the company to conduct the interview has become more important.

Levels of Communication During the Interview

What takes place between two people who meet so that one can evaluate the other and determine if he should be hired?

The interviewer is in a position of power, and the applicant is in a subordinate or dependent position. They are not on equal terms. Psychological research and common sense suggests that the individual who is being evaluated is likely to feel defensive. He will want to cover flaws and put whatever "spin" on his responses is necessary to ensure that the other person perceives him positively. Experienced interviewers will admit that even after interviewing hundreds of clients over the years, they can still be

---

[2] Anyone whose job it is to interview others for a job should inform themselves of the vast amount of information now available with respect to how we communicate non-verbally with one another through body language. A full review of this fascinating subject is beyond the scope of this book but there is much written on the topic. A good place to start might be *The Definitive Book of Body Language* by Allan and Barbara Pease published by Bantam Books in 2006).

fooled. Look between the lines of the verbal communications, read the applicant's body language , and be alert to evasiveness or attempts to gloss over some part of his background. The interview is a pressure situation—how does he handle pressure?

When a man is interviewing a woman or vice versa, the situation is more complicated than in same sex-interviews. According to Dr. Deborah Tannen, a sociolinguist specializing in the analysis of male-female communication, the communication styles of men and women are quite dissimilar.[3] Tannen notes that men tend to be more concerned with status and independence, while women tend to negotiate and seek consensus. Men are more involved with "one-up" thinking as in winners and losers; women are more concerned with feelings of community and mutual support. Thus, interviews between men and women may be seen, in Tannen's words, as "cross-cultural communications." A direct gaze from man to man may be interpreted as aggressive; from man to woman, as too forward or even flirting. Men often look outward, around the room, or at paperwork. Women look at one another when they talk. They are looking to connect, and in general, tend to be more receptive to the thoughts and feelings of others.

Male therapy interns, who are "interviewing" many hours per day in their training, initially hold to their male roles. However, with experience, they learn to use more "female" methods of communication, making eye contact more frequently without being confrontational and offering supportive words without being intrusive. Experienced male therapists are similar to women in the support they offer. They avoid one-upmanship and lecturing.

What does all this tell us? Let a woman be your lead inter-viewer, or make sure that your male interviewer (possibly, you) is in touch with his softer side.

The Wrong Candidate or a Poor Interviewer?

During a job interview, the applicant may understandably be nervous. If his nervousness results in talking too much, too little, or other seemingly inappropriate behavior, determine if this is his usual behavior or if your own clumsy interviewing technique plays a part. If the applicant's resume and references are strong, you might consider a second interview, possibly with a different interviewer if this is feasible.

If a number of interviews do not go well, consider the source: the interviewer. If you are the interviewer, have an experi-enced and trusted employee sit in with you to evaluate your style. Brush up your interviewing skill through reading, prac-tice, a class, or all of these.

The interviewer should refrain from phone calls or other inter-ruptions when talking with a candidate. A quiet room and pri-vacy are essential. Show respect to the candidate, and give him your full attention. If the interviewer fails to do this, he dilutes the importance of the meeting.

Interviewing Tips

Interviewers in training are taught not to fall into the trap of talk-ing too much. It is easy to be charmed by your own words, to want to talk about yourself and/or your company. Resist these impulses. The job interview is not a social conversation, though it may appear to be one on the surface. Rather, it is a focused set of interactions in which the questions and answers allow both parties to learn more about what they have to offer one another.

Allow the applicant time to formulate his responses and "come to you" as it were. Let him gradually open up and do as much talking as he wants. If there is a gap in the flow of conversation and the silence becomes awkward, encourage the applicant to simply "tell his story." At this point, the fewer interruptions from you the better. Pertinent information about the candidate should have been obtained either prior to the interview or at the outset. If the candidate will not or seemingly cannot develop an easy flow of conversation, this is not necessarily the end of the hiring process, but the interviewer should note this. It might be relevant to the position for which the candidate has applied.

Many interviews are performed as a two-part process. The first part is structured, and the employer asks pertinent job-related questions in a standardized manner. The second part is unstructured, and the applicant is encouraged to talk freely about people, pets, hobbies, and so on.

The questions asked (or not asked) by a candidate can be revealing. If the applicant seems primarily interested in vacation time and compensation, this says something about his needs and priorities. If he asks few questions and does not seem curious about the job or the company, this may say something about his motivation or lack of intellectual curiosity. On the other hand, a tactfully phrased question with respect to the job or the company tells you something about his social insight. Other positive flags are kind words about previous employers, an acceptance of responsibility for difficulties in a previous job, a vision of himself in your company's future, and so on. These all reveal possible strengths.

Information regarding legal aspects of hiring and firing are easily uncovered with a Google search. You must know the federal laws pertinent to hiring as well as the laws of your state. This book does not cover these laws and as the owner/employer, you are responsible for knowing them and abiding by them.

In a seminar on hiring practices, the owner of a thriving midsized business stated the following:

> *I had to get a handle on hiring. My company is not large enough to afford a full-time human resources director. Even if we could afford such a person, I don't know how much it would contribute to the bottom line. After all, how much training does it require to be able to interview applicants? So, I figured I would continue to do the interviewing.*

> *After the first seminar on interviewing, I realized that I had only been minimally prepared all these years. Probably also only minimally legal. I discovered that prior to the job interview I needed to read over the applicant's resume and jot down any questions so I wouldn't forget.*

> *Also, I learned what I could and could not ask in an interview. One thing I learned is that the main thing an interviewer should do is to listen. Be alert for inconsistencies in the applicant's story. Is the person sincere or is his story sort of pasted together to look good. Does he really want to learn and work hard and do well for himself and the company?*

An interviewer can legally ask almost any work-related questions but must be very careful with any questions that could be construed as personal.

You *can* ask these questions:

o Can the applicant perform a certain job function such as word processing?

o   Does the applicant feel that he or she can meet your company's policies with respect to work hours, vacation time, and so on?

o   What reasonable accommodations are needed if the applicant has a clear disability?

o   Does the applicant view issues such as regularity and reliability at work as important for him as they are for you? Is he okay with supervision, learning the new job? A training program?

o   What special skills does the applicant feel he has?

o   What is the applicant's prior work experience? (This is crosschecked with the background and reference material.)

o   How does the applicant see his relations with management and fellow workers in his previous job?

You *cannot* ask about the state of the applicant's health, or even whether there is any physical or mental condition on his part that would prevent him from performing the job he is applying for. You can't ask if he has AIDS, an STD, or PTSD. You can't ask what medications he may be using.

Questions about previous job-related injuries are also illegal. You can't ask the applicant to take a medical exam before you make a job offer, and you can't withdraw a job offer after you learn the results of a medical exam. (The results of any physical exam must be segregated from other personnel files and treated as confidential.) Drug testing is allowed, as are intelligence and personality testing.

To reiterate, the interviewer must be familiar with the federal, state, and local laws governing the hiring process and what is and is not allowable in an interview.

Structuring the Interview

A job interview should be opened with a few minutes of "framing"—easy conversation about the weather, sports, traffic, and so on sets a nice tone. The interviewer might then offer some structure to the situation by means of the following:

o   Offer some information about the company, its history, its status, and present focus and goals.

o   Provide some details about the job for which the candidate is being interviewed.

o   Note the approximate timeframe in which the hire is expected to take place (next month, first of the year, etc.).

o   Review the applicant's resume, possibly requesting elaboration of certain aspects of his background job experience (not his personal experience).

o   Explain other aspects of the hiring process such as drug and/or psychological testing (if these are to be used).

The interviewer should be pleasant but not overly expressive about the candidate, as unrealistic expectations may be raised. Close the interview in a friendly and respectful manner while providing a timeframe for feedback regarding the person's status.

After the interview, the interviewer should review and/or add to any notes taken during the meeting. A type of "scoring system" using a rough chart can be helpful. The chart consists of the points the interviewer wants to cover (and acts as an outline for the interview). These are checked off as the interview proceeds. Order is not important, because the conversation will usually zig and zag over different topics. An informal scoring system from a low of 1 (for a weak or poor response) to a high of 10 (for a very strong answer) may be useful. Such a procedure, or something similar of your own creation, provides a helpful "memory bank" of the interview. Adding all the scores provides a total score.

The Hypothetical Question Technique

Although the open-ended questions used by psychologists (such as "How do you feel about that?") have their uses, employers may want to be more specific. An interviewer could use real-life example questions that are job-related.

Using the hypothetical question technique, the interviewer begins by explaining that there are no right or wrong responses to the question being asked. The applicant is simply to think about the scenario presented and respond. These are "what would you do?" situations. The beauty of the technique is its flexibility. Your samples can range from delivery truck drivers to salespeople to upper-level management. You must give the same sample or samples to each candidate. Here are some hypothetical problems:

A catering firm

> *You are manager of a catering firm. This job often involves some very delicate situations with some high-strung individuals. Your firm is catering a big wedding*

53

for a wealthy, prominent family. How do you go about preparing your staff (chefs, bartenders, waitpersons) and your clients for this event, including dealing with an imperious mother of the bride and an emotional bride?

Private-public golf course

A primary problem here involves slow play and tee time mix-ups. There is also conflict between the members (who pay an extra fee for certain club tee time privileges) and members of the public, who must take whatever tee times might be available on a "first-come first-served" basis.

Think about these problems and respond to each as best you can, with it understood that you do not have all the data you might desire.

What might your strategy be with respect to the slow play? What are some of the options you would consider? What about the friction between members and non-members? How might this be reduced, if it all? What other data, if any, might you need to help make some decisions in these areas?

When possible, the interviewer should describe scenarios that either have happened or are likely to happen in the job for which the candidate has applied. The applicant's responses will reveal how he would try to resolve the problem. The way in which the individual deals with situations involving potential interpersonal friction may be brought out. Whether there has been a mature consideration of various options can be assessed, as well as whether the candidate is aware of the consequences of one decision versus another.

Because there is no way the candidate could have prepared in advance for your "problem scenario," you will get a first-hand look at how he thinks and acts under problem-solving pressure.

The hypothetical question method may not be particularly applicable for labor positions. However, if I were the interviewer for a moving van company, I would still create a few problem-solving scenes ("What pieces of furniture should be loaded first? And next?")

The mind is wonderful at vicarious thinking; we can easily dream up all sorts of problem situations. The interviewer's task is to come up with relevant, realistic problems and ask for creative and/or sensible solutions.

Something Different: The Employee Audition

The "employee audition" used by Microtraining Plus is another variation on the interview.[4] David Knise, CEO of Microtraining Plus, says, "We're hiring people for their ability to get up in front of six people they don't know and present material." Knise puts candidates on "the hot seat" by requiring them to demonstrate their skills before a final hiring decision is made. Each candidate must make an hour-long presentation to Microtraining Plus staff on any topic other than computers. Knise says, "Because we're computer people, we'd focus too much on whether what they say is right or wrong and not on their ability to teach." The technique allows management to get a first-hand look at how the individual organizes his thoughts, shows classroom command, is able to stay within time limits, and delivers information to a group in an interesting manner.

Body Language

The importance of understanding body language was briefly noted above and is reemphasized here. The body language of an appropriately self-confident candidate will project an alert, receptive, intelligent person who expects to be asked many questions, anticipates answering them, and expects to be able to ask pertinent job-related questions.[5]

Experts on body language say the following:

> In the naturally tense situation of being interviewed for a job, many people, both men and women, sit with their ankles locked. Women often lock their ankles in a way that differs from men's (e.g., hooking one foot toe down behind the other ankle). Even when a well-known model training agency advised its models not to sit with their ankles locked, too many times during an interview, when they were uncomfortable, edgy, or dissatisfied with what was happening, they locked their ankles in a most awkward way.[6]

Interviewers need to learn to look for certain gestures. Touching one's nose, for example, is a doubt sign as in, "I'm not sure I believe you," or "I'm not quite telling you the whole truth." Professor Birdwhistle of the University of Louisville noted that one of his students, when asked how he felt about a particular book, replied that he liked the book very much, touching his nose as he did so. The professor countered, "The truth is, you didn't like it." The student admitted that he had started reading the book, found it to be uninteresting, and put it down. As Nierenberg and Calero note on telling this anecdote, the student had touched his nose in front of the wrong man.[7]

The Applicant's Attire

One more thing to note on the part of the applicant is his attire. The clothes the candidate chooses for an important interview tells much about him. Depending on the culture of your company, what the applicant wears provides a clue to his perceptiveness. Has he studied your company enough to have some idea of how people dress in your workplace? If speaking with a male applicant, are his shoes shined? Did he dress appropriately (not too casual, not too formal)? If meeting with a female applicant, are her clothes too revealing? Is her skirt too short? Did she wear pants instead of a skirt? Is this in line with the culture of your company? And so on.

If the candidate can't figure out how to dress appropriately for the interview, he will probably miss other important cues in the work environment and may not "get it" in the larger picture of your company.

The interview is usually the first face-to-face contact between the company and the candidate. Even though its predictive power on the positive side is not great, its power on the negative side is high. In other words, although it is difficult to pick winners through an interview, it is easy to perceive candidates who, because of dress or behavior, are not going to fit your company culture. The interviewer must take his responsibility to the company and the candidates very seriously. Read the resumes, check the references, know exactly what the position requires, and envision how the person you are interviewing will fit into that slot.

Basic Ideas

A skillful interviewer needs to be able to put the candidate at ease, draw him out, help him explain and document his relevant work background, quickly cover what it is your company is looking for, and ascertain how the candidate sees his future with your company.

The interviewer is an important cog in the hiring process. He helps winnow out unsuitable candidates, select the most suitable applicants, and help the company move toward a hiring decision. If you as owner/manager are not a good interviewer, select someone in the company that you feel has better skills.

Interviewers may overestimate their ability to judge a candidate's future job performance. They often talk too much, and listening should be carefully cultivated.

The interviewer should maintain a courteous, professional attitude. Because men and women tend to express themselves in different ways, the interviewer needs to be aware of body language, in general, as well as gender-based communication patterns. The interview area should be quiet and private.

Because certain questions can be asked in an interview and others cannot, the interviewer needs to have exact knowledge of all relevant legal requirements.

Variations on the standard interview involve using hypothetical questions and the audition technique. The hypothetical question technique (remember, same question to each candidate) is versatile, and different "problem situations" can be devised that relate to the job being sought. The audition technique provides a good look at a candidate's performance with unfamiliar material.

The interviewer should take notes during the interview and complete them immediately afterward. All candidates should be asked the same questions and treated in a scrupulously fair manner.

CHAPTER NINE

Testing

American anti-intellectualism will never be the same because of Bill Gates. The Microsoft chief embodies what was supposed to be impossible-a practical intellectual. He consistently has sought out and hired the smartest individuals… he always hires 'brilliant' if he can… the deliberate way in which he has fashioned an organization that prizes smart people is the single most important, and the most deliberately overlooked, aspect of Microsoft's success, [1]

Randall Stross, *The Microsoft Way*

That the word intelligence describes something real and that it varies from person to person is as universal and ancient as any understanding about the state of being human. Literate cultures everywhere and throughout history have had words for saying that some people are smarter than others. Given the survival value of intelligence, the concept must be still older than that. Gossip about who in the tribe is cleverest has probably been a topic of conversation around the fires since fires, and conversation, were invented. [2]

Richard Herrnstein and Charles Murray,
The Bell Curve

> *Intelligence is the aggregate or global capacity of the individual to act purposefully, to think rationally and to deal effectively with his environment.* [3]
>
> David Wechsler, *The Measurement of Adult Intelligence, Third Ed.*

Part I

Intelligence Testing

The single best predictor of after-hire job performance in most jobs is the applicant's score on a valid intelligence test. [4] From the business person's standpoint, the importance of an intelligence test score is that it "… provides quantitative insight into how easily individuals can be trained, how well they can adjust and solve job problems, and how well-satisfied they are likely to be with job demands. Higher scoring individuals are more likely to learn more effectively from on-the-job experience and gain more from formalized training. Modest scoring individuals will require more detailed instruction, hands on practice, more time and repetition and close supervision." [5]

In general, the higher-level positions in a company deal with the more complex problems. These positions require more intelligent individuals. How do we find such people? How are they evaluated?

Intelligence testing can be as quick and simple as the twelve-minute Wonderlic Personnel Test or as extensive as the ninety-minute Wechsler Adult Intelligence Test, Fourth Edition. The Wonderlic can be administered, scored, and interpreted by the employer in office. It is so easy and inexpensive to use as a before-hire tool that there is no excuse not to use it or some equivalent test. The Wechsler, on the other hand, is a more elaborate undertaking, requiring professional administration and interpretation, and is usually used only in an extensive executive search.

Business managers move toward intelligence and personality testing because the cost of a "bad hire" is too high. One employer who had always relied on the interview and background check exclusively to make hiring decisions has now added testing to his selection process. This man states, "I interview fifteen people. I end up hiring three. One turns out to be good, the other so-so, and the other I hope quits and finds another job since it's too expensive to go through the actual process of firing him. I'm batting .333. That would get me a million dollars in pro baseball, but it's costing me a bundle in my business. I hope the testing helps."

Microsoft's penchant for "hiring the brightest" no matter the job category is interesting but may not be the best path for every company. Most companies would probably be better off spending some time carefully defining the various job categories and hiring the best and brightest applicants for the particular position, while factoring in considerations of personality (see the next section). An applicant may be "too bright" for a given job and leave for a more challenging position in another company as soon as she can. A person who fits the intellectual profile for a certain position may, in Peter Principle fashion, when promoted or sent off to a training program, not have the "smarts" for the next step forward. [3] These kinds of situations can be partially avoided by using hiring bands that define upper and lower level scores for a given position.

---

[2] The Peter Principle: In a hierarchy, every employee tends to rise to his or her level of incompetence. From, *The Peter Principle: why things always go wrong.* Buccaneer Books: New York, 1996.

What Is a Hiring Band?

A hiring band is the suggested minimum and maximum IQ scores for a job category. Every company creates its own hiring bands relative to a given job category in that company. Wonderlic provides some useful starting points for doing this. The 12 minute fifty question Wonderlic Personnel Test is scored from a low of 0 (the test-taker got no questions correct), to a high of 50 (the test-taker got all questions correct). These scores have been correlated with Wechsler Adult Intelligence Scale IQ scores (the gold standard of IQ tests). A score of 20 on the Wonderlic, for example, corresponds to an IQ score of 100 on the Wechsler test (90 to 109 is considered the average range for the adult population in the United States). The average Wonderlic score for a high school graduate is 21, in the average range of intelligence; the average for a college graduate is 29, well above average.

The Wonderlic company suggests minimum cut scores for a host of occupations. The minimum score for a secretary, for instance, is set at 25; for a warehouse worker, 17; for an attorney, 29; and so on. These may be regarded as useful guides, and they are seen as the lower edge of the hiring band.

The hiring band user has an upper limit to consider, also, and employers should not go too high above the low score. If the low score for a secretary is set at 25, we arbitrarily say that the high score (upper edge of the hiring band) is set at 29. This is not an empirically derived score. It is a guess. We are guessing that anyone applying for the position of secretary who scores below 25 or above 29 may not be smart enough for the job or, alternatively, may be too bright. If the latter, the concern is that the person will not be challenged by the work. This can often be resolved by frank discussion with the candidate.

Over a period of time, as many candidates are tested for various jobs, a company builds its own set of hiring bands. An employer gradually comes to know what the hiring band is for the jobs offered from year to year.

Is It Okay to Test?

Some years ago, IQ tests were accused of cultural bias and ran afoul of the civil rights movement. These claims were ultimately shown to be untrue for some tests; corrections were made in others to rid them of bias either for or against various racial groups. [6] Dr. Linda Gottfredson of the University of Delaware continues to make important contributions in this area. [8] Any tests of intelligence or personality offered to a business by a reputable publisher will include documentations of their courtroom legality. When in doubt, consult an attorney.

What Tests Should We Use?

The Wonderlic tests of intelligence and personality are reliable, valid, inexpensive, and easy to use. The use of the Wonderlic Personnel Test and hiring bands has been discussed above. The use of one of the Wonderlic personality tests, The Comprehensive Test of Personality, will be discussed in the next section.

Full disclosure. Although I have used its tests for years, I have no affiliation with the Wonderlic Company. I purchase their tests from the catalog, just as any business would do.

Part II

Personality Testing

Modern personality tests will generally exceed the interview and resume review in terms of after-hire job prediction. They come close to being as effective as good intelligence tests in that regard.

"Personality" may be said to refer to factors within people such as gregariousness, introversion, moodiness, shyness, and so on that are essentially genetic aspects of a person's biochemical makeup. This makeup determines the general mood, pace, and intensity of a person's behavior. Personality also includes the interpersonal strategies that the individual has developed to deal with other people and situations.

The so-called Type A personality, for example, is considered to have a high degree of drive and intensity. Although adaptive in many instances, the Type A's intensity may cause difficulty when working with others. Asking a high-drive individual to work closely with a more "laid-back" person can be a recipe for trouble, and productivity on the job can suffer.

In the same vein, hiring someone who requires a high degree of independence to work under a manager with a high need for control calls for careful consideration prior to the hire. The head of a company is usually at the helm because of certain factors having to do with intelligence *and* personality. People who are content to work under someone else generally have a personality profile that differs from the more entrepreneurial or risk-taking personality type. If personality tests are used, it is important that the employer (and other managers) complete personality profiles of themselves as well as of potential new hires.

Today, personality tests are sophisticated. They are difficult to fake, as they contain lie detectors that are not obvious. If a lie scale is triggered, the test may be invalid, and the employer might consider ending the hiring process with that candidate. When using personality tests, the applicant should be told in advance to answer each question truthfully and not try to second guess or "fake out" the test.

No personality type is inherently any better or worse than another, but some types are better suited to certain conditions than others. Although you may generally lean toward high drive, goal-oriented individuals, a calmer, more people-oriented type may actually handle the job in question better. As the employer or hiring agent, consider such factors as they emerge in the process of hiring.

Personality testing has been found to be valid, reliable, and useful in terms of assisting hiring for businesses. A recent article in one of the most prestigious psychological journals, *The American Psychologist*, concluded:

> *First, a surprising number of people still believe that personality measures are unsuitable for use in pre-employment screening... we have tried to show that these criticisms are less serious than generally believed.*
>
> *Second, we present data showing that scores on well-developed measures of normal personality are*
>
> > *a) stable over reasonably long periods of time and*
> >
> > *h) predict important occupational outcomes.*
>
> *Third, we want to suggest in the strongest possible terms that the use of well-constructed measures of normal personality in pre-employment screening will be a force for equal employment opportunity, social justice, and increased productivity.*

> *Finally, although we believe that personality measurement is appropriate for most pre-employment decisions, it should always be used in conjunction with other information, particularly in regards to the applicant's technical skills, job experience, and ability to learn.* [9]

Personality tests can be useful to an organization with a large number of job openings and when people are hired on a more or less continuous basis (e.g., a fast-food establishment). In addition to an IQ test, the company might want to use a test that measures integrity, reliability, and the ability to handle a stressful workload, because these measures tend to predict turnover, accidents, and absenteeism. To have an adequate applicant flow (and to fill the jobs as they come open), the company should consider using relatively moderate cutoff scores.

On the other hand, if your organization has many applicants for few openings, consider setting the standards higher and attempting to identify the "excellent" candidates as opposed to merely screening out marginal ones. In all cases, the personality should fit the job to be performed. For example, sales typically require a more outgoing personality. For an insurance claim investigator, you might prefer someone with a low level of trust in others, and managers need to be assertive but not overly aggressive.

The Tests in Action

There are many ways to use test results. The employer can administer IQ and personality tests that can either be sent to the test publisher to be scored or scored in the office. The employer and upper management gradually develop an understanding of and familiarity with the test results as they relate to their company. Another option is using a psychological consultant: the tests are administered by an administrative assistant and sent to the consultant for scoring and write-up. Below, we see the results of such a relationship with a consultant.

A claims management company consisting of some two dozen carefully chosen individuals, called adjustors in the parlance of the business, routinely tests candidates. The prospective employees are tested only after they have cleared the hurdles of a resume, reference checks, and an initial interview. Following testing, an individual is either dropped as a candidate or invited for a follow-up interview. The direction of this second interview draws heavily on the test results, while taking into account the findings of the other tools.

The tests are administered in the company's offices by an assistant who follows the exact protocol suggested by the company that publishes the tests and by the consulting psychologist who scores and interprets the tests. The final report is returned to the company to be scrutinized by a management team focusing on growing the company through judicious hiring.

HireSmart

Cognitive and Personality Summary

Prepared for the ABC Claims Management Company by
James Gardner, Ph.D

Name of Candidate: Mr. John Doe
Position Applied For: Claims Adjustor
Date of Testing   _____
Date of Report   _____

Cognitive Functioning

On the Wonderlic Personnel Test, Mr. Doe obtained a score of 12 under timed conditions (12 minutes), moving this up to 33 under extended time conditions (an additional 40 minutes).[1] The suggested scoring band for ABC in the job category, Adjustor, has been set at 25+. Thus, the candidate's score is essentially unacceptable for the position when time is a factor, though he is quite strong when provided with virtually unlimited time in which to work.

In effect, Mr. Doe took 52 minutes to complete a 12-minute test. If time is not a major factor in Mr. Doe's work, he clearly thinks well and is quite intelligent enough for the job; on the other hand, if time is of the essence, Mr. Doe's cognitive processing may be too slow. Because he will be working out of a home office and presumably allowed his own pace, the time factor may not be overly important. And, inasmuch as there is probably some assigned caseload with which adjustors must keep up, Management will quickly learn whether Mr. Doe, working on his own case material, can get the job done in a timely manner. The question, then, is not whether he is bright enough; it is whether he is quick enough to suit the needs of the company.

Personality Profile

This summary is based on Mr. Doe's responses to the Comprehensive Personality Profile (CPP).

---

[1] The test administrator had been trained to use this extended time procedure because it often results in richer data, as it did in this case.

The CPP provides a useful Accuracy Index in terms of responses to its various items. This index is as follows:

High Accuracy	7 to 10
Questionable Accuracy	4 to 6
Low Accuracy	0 to 3

Mr. Doe's Accuracy Index score of 10 indicates a frank and direct response to the CPP test items. Therefore, the scores on the CPP are considered to be a good reflection of the candidate's personality.

An "ABC Profile" (based on a small sample of adjustors whose work the company found to be highly satisfactory) suggested the pattern on the left below:

ABC Profile	Mr. Doe's Profile
Supporter	Supporter/Driver/Motivator
High Assertive	High Assertive
High Independent	High Independent
High Decisive	Moderate to High Decisive
High Empathy	Moderate Empathy
High Intuition	High Intuition

As can be seen, Mr. Doe's personality profile is a close match to the "ABC pattern." Unlike that pattern, however, in which the principal personality pattern was seen as a Supporter type, Mr. Doe has described himself as able to function under several of the personality profiles, presumably as the need/situation arises.

These major personality types are described as follows:[2]

Supporters

Supporters are characterized by high degrees of interpersonal warmth and patience. They tend to be even-paced, consistent, open and honest. Warmth and sensitivity to the needs of others are the Supporter's greatest strengths; a main weakness is that others often take advantage of their time and generosity. They become stressed when others demand change without giving them significant forewarning.

Drivers

Drivers are characterized by a low need for close interpersonal relationships and by a high activity level. These are the "workaholics" of the world. Drivers emphasize time management and do not tolerate inefficiency. A weakness for this type of personality may be the intolerance of and impatience with individuals who cannot keep up with their pace or make decisions quickly. Business ownership or upper-level management positions should provide the activity and direct results necessary to keep Drivers from feeling restricted.

Motivators

These individuals are easily recognized by their free-flowing, highly expressive communication skills. They enjoy any type of social interaction and like meeting new people and exploring new places. They thrive on variety and change. A principal weakness is impulsivity coupled with the need to service

---

[2] These are condensed from the CPP Manual. The manual offers more extensive comments.

everyone else's needs to the point of impeding their own job duties. They may have difficulty setting priorities. Because they are easily bored, they may have difficulty staying with a repetitive task.

Specific Personality Traits

Mr. Doe was in the Very High to High range on the following scales:

Assertiveness (84%)

Can confidently assert themselves when necessary and, in Mr. Doe's case, can probably do so without becoming overly aggressive (his score on the Aggressive scale is moderate).

Mr. Doe also scored on the high side in terms of Intuition, Independence, Objectivity, and Decisiveness.

He scored low on two scales:

Recognition Motivation (23%)	Is recognition independent and may not be particularly motivated by such things as praise or awards
Trust (33%)	Tends to be a private, even skeptical person

Management Performance Traits

Mr. Doe's profile was moderate to high on the following attributes:

> *Ability to make unpopular decisions*
> *Decisiveness to act without precedent*

71

Vision to plan ahead
Ability to be diplomatic and cooperative
Can communicate with frankness and humility
Can cope with change or disruption well

Potential Management Concerns

1. Mr. Doe's low need for recognition will require Management to determine what motivates him (kudos, pay bonuses, etc.) and provide this when feasible.

2. A low degree of trust can work well in a position such as Adjustor. However, it also can profoundly affect the employee/employer relationship unless critiques are carefully handled. Management must realize that this individual is probably somewhat distrustful and skeptical of the intentions of the Manager. Therefore, the Manager must be definitive, open and explicit in the communication process. Criticism must be constructive and well-based.

3. Mr. Doe is quite assertive, even dominant. This may present problems with clients and/or fellow workers. It seems likely that this tendency is under control, but Management will need to be alert here.

4. Mr. Doe's high intuition may sometimes result in a kind of "flying by the seat of the pants" behavior in terms of scheduling, record keeping, and so on. Again, Management will need to be alert. Possibly helping him set up a home office structure in advance would be useful.

Conclusions

A first concern about Mr. Doe is his performance on the Personnel Test. As indicated, he is bright enough, but is he fast enough? Mr. Doe, as the saying goes, grinds slowly but grinds well. Management will need to ascertain the degree of independent cognitive work involved in the job and be alert to potential time management problems.

A second concern is the fact that Mr. Doe's responses to the CPP cause him to fit in several major personality groups. This is a kind of "all things to all people" approach but, given the high Validity indicator on the CPP, it may be that this is an accurate reflection of this individual's personality. In which case, Mr. Doe is seen as a chameleon-like personality who can change to suit the demands of the situation—at times supportive, at other times, more driven. Mr. Doe has other personality traits that would seem to be ideal for the Adjustor job: namely, his low degree of trust and his no-nonsense approach to controlling the actions of others, as well as his apparent ability to work independently.

My conclusion: Probably a good hire because Management is going in knowing what to watch out for, how to train and supervise, and the cognitive limitations (very bright but very slow) in terms of working speed.

The report above was generated from the Wonderlic Personnel Test and the Comprehensive Personality Profile (CPP) by the same company. The CPP generates an extensive printout that someone in the company, or a psychological consultant, must condense to the information provided above. Creating a useful report can be somewhat daunting initially but becomes easier with practice.

At a minimum, a company should use both intelligence and personality tests, and blend the data with information from the other major tools (interview, resume review and reference checks).

Given the continued drop in the quality of the available workforce, businesses will have little choice but to look even more carefully at candidates by using their most effective selection tool: testing.

Basic Ideas

The single best predictor of after-hire job success is the applicant's score on a valid intelligence test. However, for certain positions such as sales, personality testing may be en even stronger predictor.

Used together, these tools are very strong predictors of job success. When combined with the hiring tools previously discussed—resume, references, and an interview—the employer maximizes the probability of making a good hire.

Tests for reliability, integrity, and honesty have been developed and found to be valid and useful.

Although testing is a powerful pre-employment tool, many businesses either do not use tests at all or do not consider them an overly important facet of the hire. In the future, more businesses will move toward using tests because of the expense and difficulty in finding high-quality candidates from a shrinking talent pool.

Testing is inexpensive and contributes significantly to the chances of making a good hire. Ideally, a testing program should be designed and supported by a professional who is knowledgeable of testing, the laws governing testing, and the culture of the company.

CHAPTER TEN

Linking

B y the time an employer has reviewed the resume of an applicant, checked his background, interviewed him, and run cognitive and personality tests, he has invested considerable time and money in this one candidate. He has also amassed a great deal of data that must be condensed and point to an informed hire/no-hire decision. As we have seen, a bad hire costs money and is frustrating. Companies need to make the most of their data and make a good hire.

The four hiring tools mentioned here are sometimes not used, and using the bare minimum of an application review and a cursory interview, the employer will hire a "winner." This could happen with the first person who applies for the job or one of the first three or four applicants. The employer does not realize that he has lucked out. He thinks that this is what it's all about: advertise for the job, review the resume, do a quick interview, and hire someone. Finding a winner in this way is like hitting a great golf shot once or twice per round or hitting the jackpot in a casino. You can do it now and then, but you can't do it with any consistency.

Once an employer becomes accustomed to what is essentially a haphazard hiring procedure, he will rarely abandon it. It works for him on an intermittent basis, and likely he does not know a better way. On the other hand, the employer with a full arsenal of hiring tools will hire better people more often.

To match an applicant's skills with the job you want filled, the position should be well defined. Titles such as *clerk, secretary*, or *sales rep* are typical but vague. An effective, specific job description might be as follows:

Executive Assistant Wanted

> *This position requires excellent communication skills, including the ability to write well. Tact and sensitivity are prerequisites, yet the successful candidate will be sufficiently assertive to be able to schedule the executive's calendar while dealing positively with the demands of others to be included on that schedule. The successful applicant will be able to organize meetings and seminars and perform other duties commensurate with smooth executive performance within a large organization*

The "other duties commensurate with smooth executive performance" is vague, but otherwise the ad succinctly describes what is needed.

Once a good job description has been developed, the employer's hiring decision becomes easier; the candidate either does or does not fit the needs of the position. Employers hire the person who most closely approximates that fit. Assessing the candidate's skills is a process that requires ongoing linking between the different forms of information at your disposal.

Many jobs require multitasking skills. For example, an employee may, at different times, sell to prospects, buy goods or material for the company, review contracts, or supervise other employees. The preferred worker in some jobs is not a narrow specialist but rather an intelligent generalist who can handle several different tasks simultaneously.

After a job description has been developed and ads are placed in relevant job forums, be prepared to receive applications. The subsequent tasks are more or less as follows:

1. The employer or manager reads and reviews the resumes submitted by the candidates.

2. If the basic form has been adequately filled out and the information appears to match the job advertised, interviews are scheduled.

3. Prior to the interview, the employer formulates some questions:

> *a. What is my impression of this candidate based on this initial contact?*
>
> *b. How accurate is the information provided? For example, was the applicant really a "supervisor," or did he decide that he watched as a job was being done and "sort of supervised" it?*
>
> *c. Was the position the candidate previously held at XYZ Company closely similar to the one he is applying for or at least somewhat similar? (Underline this and make a note to explore it further in an interview.)*

The employer should be alert to matches or mismatches in the resume, especially unexplained time gaps during which the person was possibly not employed.

4. References are checked. Ask each of the previous employers the same set of questions, and ask the all-important question: Would you hire this person for that position again?

5. If the applicant is still a candidate, schedule an interview.

6. Depending on the importance of the job involved, use one or more of the interview techniques discussed in Chapter Eight. If the interview is positive, schedule testing.

7. Review the candidate's test scores. Is the candidate sufficiently bright for the job? Too bright? Does the candidate's personality profile match up with the personality type you feel is needed for the job? If not, this is something to consider but may not rule the candidate out. He may become a valuable employee but may need some initial training and supervision.

In a discussion with me, the owner of a midsized company (fifty to sixty employees) states:

> I have learned to look for discrepancies (in the data), not so much to find fault with the candidate but to be as sure possible that if I hire him I am going to place this person in as good a position as possible to help my company. The open position here in my company does not require a high level of verbal ability. It is not a sales job, but you do have to communicate. The applicant communicated very adequately in the interview but was not brilliant. Actually, I don't need 'brilliant.' I need competency and reliability. There is every indication from the background check that the applicant is both of these.
>
> Smart enough? The testing is going to tell me that. I look at the applicant's problem-solving skills as revealed by the test. Does the score indicate that this person fits the hiring band for the job category? If not, what to do? If the

score is close enough, I'd probably hire anyway. Good people are hard to find. If the score is too low, though, I'd be wary. At the end of all this, we think we are going to get a person who will be able to do the job well. A person who will become a productive part of what we think is a very strong workforce.

The sheer amount of data generated by the four hiring tools on just one candidate can seem overwhelming at first glance. This may cause an "analysis paralysis" reaction. Where to start? What to do with all of this information?

Begin by sorting your data bit by bit. Think about the demands of the position. Review the candidate's background and browse the references and resume once more. Reflect on the person's performance in the interview. Look at the intelligence and personality test scores. Jot down your own informal scores, assigning 1 to 5 for each of the four areas (or five areas if you divide the test score between the intelligence and the personality tests). If another person is sharing the hiring duties with you, comparing impressions and scores will be highly useful. What areas do you agree or disagree on?

You have linked your data. You are moving toward your probable best hire, and it all becomes easier with practice.

Basic Ideas

Using all four tools generates a great deal of information. Combining the information gleaned from the tools is done by "linking."

Synthesizing and summarizing the data can be a bit overwhelming and can result in "analysis paralysis." Review the data, and discuss it with a colleague. An informal scoring system can be useful.

Every employer engages in linking to some extent with every hire. This is at both conscious and subconscious levels. It ranges from going through the data in an almost point-by-point manner to simply "having a gut feeling" about the candidate after reviewing the results of the hiring tools.

It can be said that all employers use two of the four hiring tools available: the application/resume and the interview. Some add reference checks. Others, probably still a minority among small to midsized businesses, add testing and thus do the most thorough job possible in the hiring selections.

When an organization needs a position to be filled, two kinds of diagnostic procedures are necessary: a careful job description and a thorough assessment of the candidate. The person and the job must have a good "fit."

CONCLUSION

I am told that writers often reluctantly leave a subject that interests them and on which they have been working. I leave this book reluctantly. Even so, I feel that I have said what I wanted to say about the interesting topic of the selection of people to enhance one's workforce: hiring.

As I was putting the finishing touches on this book, an article in the April 5, 2011 edition of *The Wall Street Journal* leapt out at me: "India Graduates Millions, but Too Few Are Fit to Hire." The article cites India's difficulties in producing high school and college graduates who are job-ready. The schools are often expensive but lax. Students just don't learn very much. Companies such as Tata and IBM go on their own recruiting forays and have set up their own after-hire training programs. I was reminded, of course, of America's deteriorating workforce.

It is my hope that we can arrest the decline of good workers and continue to produce an intelligent and educated pool of people that business can hire and train for its needs. We need to support solid K–12 schooling as well as the G. I. Bill for our returning veterans. Monies spent in these areas will be a critically important step in building a strong workforce, and a capable and competent workforce is a primary investment in our nation's future.

CHAPTER NOTES

Introduction

1. John Smith, "Four Lessons Our Airlines Need to Learn," *The Wall Street Journal*, November 6, 1993.

2. Jerry Flint, "Can You Tell Applesauce from Pickles?" *Forbes,* October 9, 1995.

3. Bill Plashke and Elliott Almont, "Has the NFL Draft Become a Thinking Man's Game?" *The Los Angeles Times*, April 21, 1995.

Chapter One

1. Jeremy Rifkin, *The End of Work* (New York: Tarcher/Putnam, 1995), 162.

Chapter Two

1. Richard Herrnstein and Charles Murray, *The Bell Curve* (New York: Free Press/Simon and Schuster, 1996), 63.

2. Howard Gardner, *Frames of Mind: The Theory of Multiple Intelligences* (New York: Basic Books, 1983).

3. Mark Snyderman and Stanley Rothman, *The IQ Controversy: The Media and Social Policy* (New Brunswick, NJ: Transaction, 1988).

4. Linda Gottfredson, "Why *g* Matters: The Complexity of Everyday Life," *Intelligence,* 24, no. 1 (1997): 79–112.

5. *Wonderlic Personnel Test User's Manual* (Libertyville, IL, 1992), 24.

6. R. D. Arvey, "General Ability in Employment: A Discussion," *Journal of Vocational Behavior* (1986), 415–420.

Chapter Three

1. Paul Gray, "Debating Standards," *Time,* April 8, 1996.
2. Ibid.
3. Editorial, "The Poor Need High Tech," *The Los Angeles Times,* May 20, 1886.
4. Louis Gertsner, Jr., "Our Schools Are Failing: Do We Care?" *The New York Times,* May 27, 1994.
5. Robert Wendover, *Smart Hiring* (Naperville, IL: Small Business Sourcebooks, 1999).
6. Ruben Navarette, Jr., "Reforming Education Should Begin in the Classroom," *The Los Angeles Times,* May 12, 1996.
7. Adrienne Mack, "Standards versus Graduation Rate: A Catch-22 Situation," *The Los Angeles Times,* June 9, 1996.
8. Editorial, "CSUN Freshmen Bring Baggage," *The Los Angeles Times,* April 14, 1996.

Chapter Four

1. Erin Davis, "Wired for Hiring: Microsoft's Slick Recruiting Machine," *Fortune,* February 5, 1996.
2. Ibid
3. R. H. Hawk, *The Recruitment Function* (New York: American Management Association, 1967).
4. Stuart Silverstein, "Job Prospects Look Hot for Geezer Boomers in 2020," *The Los Angeles Times,* April 26, 1997.
5. Anne Underwood, "Can Memory Loss Be Prevented?" *The New York Times,* June 9, 2009.

Chapter Five

1. Martin Yates, *Hiring the Best: A Manager's Guide to Effective Interviewing* (Avon, MA: Adams Media, 1994), 151.
2. J. Hunter and R. Hunter, "Validity and Utility of Alternative Predictors of Job

Performance," *Psychological Bulletin* 96 (1984): 72–98.
3. Daniel Seligman, *A Question of Intelligence: the IQ debate in America*. Citadel Press: New York, 1994.

Chapter Six
1. J. Hunter and R. Hunter. op.cit.

Chapter Seven
1. Under the 1972 Fair Credit Act, an employer needs the applicant's permission to check the references, even though the applicant herself has provided these references. Your company's application form might contain a simple statement asking for the candidate's signed permission to check the references. When a resume is presented, you might obtain signed permission directly from the candidate. As always, check with your own attorney regarding how this matter is best handled in your state.
2. Susan Dearmin, "The Art of Checking References," *Valley Business Journal*, July, 1996.

Chapter Eight
1. L. E. Tyler, *The Work of the Counselor* (New York: Appleton-Century-Croft, 1969).
2. Irving Wiener (ed.), "The Assessment Interview," *Clinical Methods in Psychology* (New York: Wiley, 1976), 3.
3. Deborah Tannen, *You Just Don't Understand* (New York: Ballantine, 1990).
4. Donna Fern, "Hiring: Employee Audition," *Inc. Magazine*, June,1966.
5. Julius Fast, *Body Language* (New York: MJF Books, 1970).
6. Gerard Nierenberg and Henry Calero, *How to Read a Person Like a Book* (New York: Barnes and Noble, 1993).
7. Ibid.

Chapter Nine

1. Michael Stross, *The Microsoft Way* (New York: Addison-Wesley, 1996).

2. Richard Hernstein and Charles Murray, op.cit.

3. David Wechsler, *The Measurement of Adult Intelligence, 3rd Ed.* (Baltimore: Williams & Williams, 1944).

4. *Wonderlic Personnel Test and Scholastic Level Exams, User's Manual* (Libertyville, IL: Wonderlic Inc., 1992).

5. ibid

6. A. Wigdor and W. Garner (eds.), *Ability Testing: Uses, Consequences and Controversies* (Washington, DC: National Academy Press, 1982).

7. Linda Gottfredson, "Reconsidering Fairness: A Matter of Social and Ethical Priorities," *Journal of Vocational Behavior* 33, no. 3 (1988), 295–319.

8. Robert Hogan, Joyce Hogan, and Brent Roberts, "Personality Measurement and Employment Decisions: Questions and Answers," *American Psychologist* (1996) 469–477.

About the author

After receiving an Honorable Discharge from the United States Army following the Korean War, Dr. James Gardner worked in private industry for several years prior to earning a doctorate degree in clinical psychology from the University of California, Los Angeles. He has held faculty teaching positions at California State University Northridge, the University of Southern California, and the University of California, Los Angeles. Prior to retirement, Dr. Gardner maintained a private practice in psychology in Brentwood, California, consulted with public and private schools, engaged in clinical research, and worked with various businesses regarding personnel selection by developing in-house testing programs. He has published three books as well as over more than two dozen papers in professional journals. Dr. Gardner's current research focus is on the enhancement of workforce effectiveness through strong selection procedures.